Y0-BCL-336

DECISIONS

SOUTHERN MISSIONARY COLLEGE
Division of Nursing Library
711 Lake Estelle Drive
Orlando, Florida 32803

DF 2016
SDA

DECISIONS

**How
To Use
Biblical
Guidelines
When
Making
Decisions**

8169

BJ
1468.5
.B 899
.1979

**by
John Brunt**

SOUTHERN MISSIONARY COLLEGE
Division of Nursing Library
711 Lake Estelle Drive
Orlando, Florida 32803

Copyright © 1979 by
Southern Publishing Association

This book was
Edited by Gerald Wheeler
Designed by Mark O'Connor

Type set: 11/13 Palatino

Printed in U.S.A.

Library of Congress Cataloging in Publication Data

Brunt, John, 1943-
   Decisions: how to use Biblical guidelines when making decisions.

   Includes bibliographical references.
   1. Decision-making (Ethics)   2. Bible—Ethics.
I. Title.
BJ1468.5.B78   241   79-16158
ISBN 0-8127-0235-2

For Ione,

whose decision to share her life with me has
made life so rich and full of joy.

Contents

Chapter 1

Is the Bible Relevant?

A group of denominational educators was visiting our campus to evaluate the college for the General Conference. Since they were particularly interested in the spiritual atmosphere of the school, they spent some time in group discussion with those of us in the religion department, asking about our curriculum and approach to teaching religion classes. During the course of the conversation one of them asked, "Are you still teaching your general students mostly Biblical courses like Life and Teachings of Jesus and Bible Doctrines, or are you offering courses more relevant to the actual decisions students have to make—courses about sex, drugs, and such?"

His question implies a dichotomy that has become quite common: *Biblical* vs. *relevant*. Many question whether the Bible actually has any significance for the kinds of decisions that we have to make in the twentieth century, and there are good reasons for such a question. Obviously the Bible does not address many of the problems that make some of today's decisions so perplexing.

For instance, the Bible never deals with the problem of abortion, but today decisions regarding abortion confront not only the women directly involved but counselors and health-care providers as well. Nor does the Bible speak directly to the problems of dating and courtship brought about by today's dating game. (How could it? In most of Biblical times parents arranged marriages and girls were married by the time they were twelve or thirteen.)

In addition, modern technology has introduced problems that would never have entered the minds of Biblical authors but at the same time, ones that demand decisions on our part. We find this particularly true in the area of medical ethics. When, for instance, is it permissible to withdraw life-support systems from a patient who appears to have no chance of conscious life?

On the other hand, the Bible does mention many problems involving moral decisions that may no longer concern us today. The Western world does not have to confront the problem of whether we should or should not eat food that someone has offered to idols, yet Paul devotes three chapters (1 Corinthians 8:1–11:1) to the subject. Most of us wouldn't even know what he was talking about without help from commentaries explaining some of the historical background.

The central question of this book is: Can we bridge the gap between Scripture and the decisions we make? Can a book written many years ago and addressing such different circumstances and problems have any value for our decision-making?* Can we be *both* Biblical and relevant?

Our thesis is that the Bible is not only pertinent but indispensable as well for Christian decision-making. We often fail to see its relevance, however, because of unrealistic expectations. We assume the Bible will give us the right answers to every dilemma, answers ready to use like the food that goes straight from the supermarket to our tables. When Scripture does not do so, we conclude that it does not apply today. But the Bible contributes to our decision-making in a much deeper and more profound way than merely providing prepackaged answers to our every dilemma.

First of all, the Bible forms the basic framework within which we make our decisions, and it shows us their significance. Knowing the context and importance of our decision-making in turn affects the way we go about making specific decisions. Chapters 2 and 3 begin our discussion by exploring the basic framework to our decision-making, which the Bible furnishes.

---

*When we speak of decision-making we are, of course, referring to decisions with moral and religious significance. Many decisions, such as which shoe to put on first in the morning or what color car to buy, lack such import. Decisions receive moral and religious value as they affect other people and our relationship with God.

Chapter 2

Faith and the Good News

The most important contribution the Bible makes to the process of decision-making is its revelation of the framework in which we stand as we make decisions. That structure is the context of God's grace. We begin with the knowledge that God has saved us, not on the basis of our actions, but of His love. The good news of the gospel is as relevant as ever. The world needs to hear it today as much as it ever has needed to hear it. Our knowledge of it has a profound effect on our decision-making. In fact, it transforms our whole understanding of the nature and significance of human action.

Let us begin with an illustration. I once saw a Sabbath School teacher in one of the children's divisions use a clever, but also dangerous and deceptive, didactic device. She had a number of small images of children, made out of metal, engaged in various activities.

Some of the children were doing "good" things (praying, reading the Bible, washing the dishes, helping an older person), while other children were doing "bad" things (fighting with other children, making a face, stealing). The children in the Sabbath School class first saw all the metal children doing their good and bad deeds, and then the teacher introduced another figure. It was a metal representation of Christ, which hid a magnet behind it. As "Christ" came down from above the table it picked up all the boys and girls who were doing good things to take them to heaven (they were steel so that the magnet would pick them up) but left behind all of the children who were doing bad things (they looked the same as the other figures, but were actually of aluminum).

Such a device gives a typical religious view of the significance of human action. According to this view, human actions come first, and God responds to them. If what we do is good, He rewards us, but if it is bad, God reacts unfavorably with punishment. Such a view makes human action the decisive ingredient in salvation. Everything rides on what we do, for God responds to our actions.

But the Christian gospel turns this concept completely upside down. It teaches that God's action comes first, and we are the respondents.

God took the initiative to save us, apart from our actions. When our actions offered nothing that would commend us to God, He Himself moved to save us. Paul makes it sure and certain that God saved us because of His love, not because of our good behavior, when he says, "But God shows his love for us in that while we were yet sinners Christ died for us" (Romans 5:8, RSV*).

Do you see how Paul's picture differs from that presented by the Sabbath School device? Now it is God who acts, and we who respond. Not that our action is worthless. God's love demands a response. Indeed how we respond to it determines our destiny.

By trusting in Him we receive life, while rejecting Him cuts us off from its source. The Lord respects man's freedom too much to force salvation on anyone. Thus we must accept His grace. Vital as human action is, it is always a *response* to what God has done *first*. He *first* loved and saved us. We are saved by His grace, His unmerited favor, not by any action that we have done, are doing, or will do in the future. We only respond to His act of salvation.

Once we recognize that only God's action saves us, we find that this has implications for the way we understand the entire endeavor of decision-making. (It also has real bearing on the specific decisions that we make, but that will be the topic of Chapter 4.)

First, knowing that salvation is by God's grace rather than by our doing means that the decisions we make and the actions we subsequently perform we never do to earn His favor, for we already have it. In one sense, this takes some of the pressure off our decision-making. We know that God is not waiting to zap us the first time we make a wrong decision or perform a wrong act. He is already for us from the beginning. Thus we are free to proceed with the assurance that our actions are not the essential ingredient in salvation, but that salvation depends rather on what God has already done.

But second (and it may sound paradoxical at first), rather than minimize the importance of our decisions and actions, their context of God's grace gives them a new and greater value, for they become expressions of our response to His love for us. That which God has done for us places even greater responsibility on us.

When we understand the magnificence of His free grace, it intensifies the desire to respond appropriately, and we care more than ever about our actions. Thus while it abolishes the effort to earn God's favor, it at the same time awakens the desire to reveal our love for Him and our trust in Him through our conduct. The net result is *re-sponsi*bility, in which we take our actions seri-

ously because we see them as an expression of
our response to God.

Third, by the Good News of God's grace our
actions acquire a certain relativity—*not* the kind
which says that since all things are relative, it
doesn't really matter what you do. Not at all. But
what is of ultimate significance is not our specific
decisions and acts, *as such*, but the way that our
actions express our response to God. The way we
acknowledge our relationship with God is more
important than the rightness or wrongness of
specific actions.

What God looks for is our trust in Him and the
acceptance of His gift. Although our response is
seen in our actions, it also transcends specific
ones. The essential ingredient in salvation is not
the performance of certain actions but a certain
kind of relationship with our Saviour. Here we
see the relativity of our actions—actions are relative to our relationship with God. Thus our all-
too-frequent question "Is _____
(You can fill in the blank with all kinds of
specifics I am sure) right or wrong?" is too shal-
low. We must go on to ask, "How does this
specific action in my particular circumstances
express my trust in God and affect my relationship with Him?"

Therefore the question of *motive* is of crucial
importance in the process of Christian

decision-making. We must consider not only the "what" but also the "why." The same action may or may not express one's faith in God. The identical action might be a vehicle of trust in God or rejection of Him, depending upon the motive that prompted it. For instance, I might give to the poor because I genuinely appreciate God's gift of grace, or because I want to impress everyone with my piety so that I can exalt myself.

But the relativity of human action has still another aspect. The New Testament makes it clear that there exists an integral connection between my relationship with God and my relationship with others. The appropriate response to God's grace is love for His other children. (We will say more about this in Chapter 4.) Thus specific actions are also relative to the effect they have on others. Therefore the *consequences* of actions have crucial significance in the process of Christian decision-making. In 1 Corinthians 8:13 Paul shows that actions which might be quite legitimate in themselves might be quite wrong if they would serve to harm another person.

All of this tells us that Christian action (and thus Christian decision-making) never takes place in a vacuum. It is never simply the individual and his action that is in view but the relationship of the individual to God and to others. Such relationships determine the significance of a specific action. Thus the first great commandment is love to God, and the second is love for the neighbor. The Christian's ultimate question is never simply the rightness or wrongness of actions in the abstract. The Christian must always concern himself with actions as they relate to God and others.

Fourth and finally, the framework of God's grace influences Christian decision-making by speaking to human existence on a level that goes beyond simply discovering what is right and wrong. It reminds us of the problem of human weakness. Usually we think of the dilemma of deciding what is right or wrong, but so often our real difficulty is that we fail to do even that which we know to be right.

We have all felt the frustration of Romans 7:19, in which Paul says, "I do not do the good I want, but the evil I do not want is what I do." All of us have found it much easier to make decisions about what we should do in the form of resolutions than to actually carry them out.

Our human weakness confronts us at an early age. One Friday afternoon when my children were about seven and five they went to the store with me while I did the grocery shopping. When we returned home and got out of the car my arms were full of groceries. "Please close the door," I asked them. I made the fatal mistake, however, of failing to specify which child, and they started arguing. Each wanted to do it without the help of the other. Finally Laura gave Larry a shove and quickly closed the door. Larry retaliated by grabbing big sister's arm and sinking his teeth into it. At that point it was time for Dad to step in, and both received punishment in proportion to their crime.

A couple of hours later they met again for the first time as we sat down for dinner. Larry was repentant. He looked at Laura and said, "I'm sorry I bit you. I won't ever do it again. I'm going to be good clear till Jesus comes. . . ." And then, recognizing all too well the dilemma of human weakness, he added, ". . . if I remember."

His sister, who still had teeth marks in her arm, responded with disgust, "You won't."

How typical it was of the human predicament. The spirit is willing, but the flesh is weak. But the Good News that the Bible reveals speaks to our dilemma in two ways.

First, it offers us God's forgiveness. The Good News is that He is forgiving—He does not hold our mistakes against us. We face the future with assurance because we know that we need never let the awareness of our past mistakes crush us. Thus, freed from anxiety and guilt, decision-making can proceed in an atmosphere of confidence.

✗ Second, God freely offers power for the future by providing us with the motivation to carry out our convictions. Such strength comes as the awareness of His love for us changes our character. The analogy of human love helps us understand this power.

I think, for instance, of a young boy shipped around from home to home. He had never known a stable, loving environment, and this background had taken its toll. It was easy to see the anger and aggression that dominated his play with other children. Then something happened that made all the difference. The social workers placed him in a home in which people genuinely loved him. He learned to trust the new mommy and daddy who cared for him with such loving patience. The transformation was amazing. Love had the power to change the life.

In the same way, God's love is the power that transforms the life of the sinner. Often we get the idea that if we can just convince people how wretched they are by sufficient verbal spankings, they will change. But the power to alter lives comes in the Good News of God's love. The gospel is, as Paul says, "the power of God for salvation to every one who has faith" (Romans 1:16).

Therefore the Bible speaks to Christian

decision-making at a level that goes beyond the problem of choosing what is right and wrong. It addresses the true human dilemma, that of human weakness. If we put the Bible aside and simply concentrate on decision-making, no matter how "relevant" the decisions may be, we rob ourselves of the framework we need in order to understand what our decision-making is all about, and of the power we need to motivate us once we have made a decision.

We must view the entire decision-making process within the context of God's grace, and it is the Good News of God's grace that has the power to change the heart. Without such a framework we misunderstand the significance of our decision-making and see it as that which is ultimate. We may make decisions, but our decison-making will be Christian only when it becomes a part of our response to God's free gift.

So far we have seen that the Bible is not only relevant but also actually indispensable to Christian decision-making, because it reveals to us the context of God's grace. If we ever put all our eggs in the basket of trying to make right decisions about "relevant" issues without concentrating on the framework of God's grace in which we stand as we make those decisions, we risk losing our grasp of the significance of our decision-making and our actions. We could forget that our source of strength and life lies in God's grace rather than our actions.

---

*All Scripture quotations unless otherwise indicated are taken from the Revised Standard Version.

Chapter 3

Why Not Just Obey?

Recently I heard someone say that the nice thing about being a Seventh-day Adventist is you always know just what to do. If you face a dilemma for which the Bible does not provide the right answer, you can at least find it in the writings of Ellen G. White.

I am afraid, however, that statement is an oversimplification. True, we often think of Christian decision-making as simply a matter of going to what God has revealed and finding the right answer to every specific problem. We assume that it is not really for us to decide what to do but rather for us to obey. After all, our own weak and sinful reason is hardly competent to show us what we should do. We need answers given from above. Our task is to find the correct one in God's Word, and then do what it says.

But such a view of Christian decision-making does not square with what we have seen in the last chapter. The fact that specific actions are relative to our relationships with God and others forces us to look beyond just determining whether they are right or wrong. As we saw, we must consider motives and consequences of actions as well. The significance of an action will differ in various circumstances, depending on the network of relationships involved. Every incident differs. Thus what may sound like a right answer to my dilemma may not be appropriate for another's. Responsible Christian action varies with time, place, culture.

One of the clearest Biblical examples occurred when Paul discussed the problem of food offered to idols in 1 Corinthians 8:1–11:1, and a closer look at that passage will give us insight.

The Corinthian believers had written Paul a letter in which they had asked several questions about specific actions—were they right or wrong? One question concerned food presented to idols. At that time most of the food found in the marketplace had been sacrificed to an idol by consecrating a portion of the food in the temple. The people believed that in this way the protection of the god or goddess passed on to the one who ate the food. In addition, many of the banquets and ordinary social occasions took place in the temple, and at such occasions they would definitely sacrifice a portion of the food to one of

the pagan gods. How should Christians relate to
the practice?

Paul's answer is complex. He refuses to answer with a simple "It is right" or "It is wrong."
His ethical thinking went beyond the "right answer" approach. The apostle recognized that the
significance of the act of eating food offered to
idols might differ, depending on the circumstances.

Also Paul knew that in a church made up of
people of diverse backgrounds one must consider the entire network of relationships between them. To simply second the practice of one
group might lead them to pride and thus further
polarize the already-divided church. More than a
yes or no was needed, for more was at stake than
the rightness or wrongness of the act of eating
food presented to idols.

Thus Paul confirms that since an idol has no
real existence, the mere act of consuming food
offered to an idol can do no harm. One is no
better or worse off by whether he/she does or
does not eat (8:4-6, 8). But he also warns that the
knowledge of that fact might lead to arrogance. In
addition, some have been so much in the habit of
worshiping idols in the past that they could not
eat now with a clear conscience. They would still
make a connection in their minds between the
food and the idol, and for them to eat would be

wrong (verse 7).

Thus an act perfectly legitimate in itself became wrong for some people because of their cultural and religious background. Such a background made it impossible for them to perform that specific act with the proper motives.

But Paul goes further. Those Christians who realize that food dedicated to idols cannot affect them have a responsibility to the "weak." If the example of those who have knowledge injures the weak, the former have not acted in love. Thus again an act perfectly legitimate might be wrong, but now for different reasons, not because of their own thinking but because of its effect upon others. It is wrong not because of anything inherent in the act itself but because of its consequences.

Thus Paul tells the Corinthians who possess knowledge, "Only take care lest this liberty of yours somehow become a stumbling block to the weak. For if any one sees you, a man of knowledge, at table in an idol's temple, might he not be encouraged, if his conscience is weak, to eat food offered to idols? And so by your knowledge this weak man is destroyed, the brother for whom Christ died. Thus, sinning against your brethren and wounding their conscience when it is weak, you sin against Christ. Therefore, if food is a cause of my brother's falling, I will never eat meat, lest I cause my brother to fall" (verses 9-13).

In chapter 9 Paul gives a personal example of his own willingness to forfeit his legitimate rights for the sake of others. He has the right to receive financial support in spreading the gospel, but he chooses not to accept it so that he will not put any obstacle in the way of the gospel of Christ. Finally, after three chapters of laying down the principles that must govern such a decision, Paul is ready to give some specific advice on the use of food offered to idols. Christians may eat whatever sells in the meat market without asking questions.

Here it is a private matter that will not affect others, and thus the act itself causes no harm. Since the idol is nothing, the eating of food consecrated to it cannot change one's relationship to God (10:25, 26). Paul also advises that the Christian invited to a nonbeliever's home should eat the meat that the host sets before him without asking whether or not it had been offered to idols.

But again, the significance of the action may change depending on the influence it will have on others. If someone tells him/her that a certain food has been offered to idols, he/she should refrain for the sake of the other person (10:27-29).

Paul concludes the discussion by summarizing the basic principle that must motivate the

Christian's decision on the question under consideration: "So, whether you eat or drink, or whatever you do, do all to the glory of God. Give no offense to Jews or to Greeks or to the church of God, just as I try to please all men in everything I do, not seeking my own advantage, but that of many, that they may be saved. Be imitators of me, as I am of Christ" (10:31–11:1).

Thus a section of Scripture discussing a question hardly relevant to our age does offer some important insights into Christian decision-making. It points to a complexity in Christian decision-making which goes beyond the question of the rightness or wrongness of a specific act.

Paul reminds us that we must consider many factors, for the significance of the act changes in different circumstances. The cultural and religious background of the person, the persons who witness the act, and the effect of the action on others are all important. That is why when the early church asked Paul, "Is it right or wrong to eat food offered to idols?" he answered neither with a yes or a no, but with, "That depends," followed by an elucidation of the kinds of principles that must govern such a decision.

Something that once happened to my wife before our marriage gives a more contemporary illustration of the changing significance of actions depending on the circumstances. When she and her girl friend were touring Europe one summer after a year of college abroad in France, they crossed the mouth of the Mediterranean Sea and visited Tangier, Africa.

They found a beach there that was much too inviting to pass up. After changing into their modest, one-piece bathing suits, they went for a swim. But they abbreviated their swim, however, when they saw that their action, which would have been perfectly normal on the beaches of Southern California, had a different significance in Tangier. Their first clue to the difference came when they realized a group of staring men followed them into the water. In fact, it included almost all the men from the beach. Then they noticed that it was *only* men who were swimming there. There were women present, but they all stood on the shore dressed in clothing that covered everything but their eyes.

It didn't take long for my wife and her friend to decide that they really didn't want to swim at that beach after all. That which would have been a perfectly responsible Christian action in another context received a new significance here, and they found themselves communicating something that they had not intended. Again we see that responsible Christian action must consider many factors of time, place, culture.

Once we grasp this complexity it becomes obvious that the law, even if we extend it to include all of the Bible, or even all of the Bible and the writings of Ellen G. White, can never cover every situation. We can never hope to have the right answer to every dilemma handed to us. Even Adventists, blessed with divine instruction, must weigh the factors, evaluate the circumstances, and think as they attempt to make decisions.

In fact, even where the law gives us specific commands, we often find that it does not define or interpret the command but leaves that task to us. For instance, the commandment says, "You shall not kill." Scholars generally agree that the Hebrew word used here means "to murder." But what is murder? While in many situations the answer to that question is quite clear, in others it is not.

What does the commandment mean for the physician who agonizes over whether or not to continue the use of life-support systems on a person who seems to have no chance of conscious existence but exists only because of the machine? The physician knows that the patient's family is running up a bill that they can ill afford. He/she is convinced that normal life will never again be possible. Yet the doctor is also committed to the preservation of life.

What is "life" in this case? And what is "murder"? Would the removal of the life-support system be "killing"? It is clear that the commandment says not to kill, but it is far from clear precisely what constitutes killing. God has left it to us to interpret the commands He has given. It is not enough simply to obey—we must think and make decisions.

But now that we have seen the complexity of the Christian's decision-making task, have seen that we cannot expect to find prepackaged answers to our every dilemma, and have seen that Christian responsibility means more than simply obeying certain commands, how are we to respond? It might be tempting to throw our hands in the air and in confusion say, "Who am I to be given such a task? If everything is relative, it would be better simply to do as I please and follow the line from the song that introduced the *Happy Days* television program: 'It feels so right it can't be wrong.' If I can't depend on God to supply the right answers, how will I ever know what to do?"

Fortunately God has not left us without guidance. In fact, He has a purpose in mind when He places the responsibility to think, interpret, and decide upon us. He could have provided us all with a Urim and Thummim that would light up to give us a simple yes or no answer to our every question. Or He could have given us a holy coin to flip whenever we were in doubt about His will for us. But He didn't. Like any wise parent He wanted to do more than teach us to obey His every command like a robot. The Lord wanted us to develop the power to think and to do, to do the right thing because we ourselves have come to recognize that it is right.

Yes, we are to obey, but our obedience is to be intelligent service, not blind obedience that cannot function in the absence of a specific command for every situation. True obedience is a matter of the heart and of the mind, not of mere external behavior. God gives us both freedom and the responsibility to use it intelligently because He wants us to develop the power to think and to do.

The advice that Ellen White gives concerning the use of signs to make decisions illustrates this point clearly. Some Christians in her day were using such methods as the flipping of coins or cards to decide the Lord's will for them. They prayed that God would lead and make the coin or card come up the right way to show them their duty. Ellen White had absolutely no sympathy for such methods, as we see in the following excerpts taken from *Selected Messages*, Book Two, pages 325-327.

"You endeavor to reach correct decisions regarding religious duties, and to make decisions regarding business enterprises, by the tossing up of a coin, and letting the position in which it falls decide what course you shall pursue. I am instructed to say that we are not to give encouragement to any such methods. They are too common, too much like sleight-of-hand movements. They are not of the Lord, and those who depend upon them for direction will meet with failure and disappointment. Being nothing more than a matter of chance, the influence of adopting such tests regarding duty is calculated to lead the mind to depend on chance and guesswork, when all our work and plans for work should be established on the sure foundation of the Word of God. . . .

"To our people I will say, Let none be led from the sound, sensible principles that God has laid down for the guidance of His people, to depend for direction on any such device as the tossing up of a coin. Such a course is well pleasing to the enemy of souls; for he works to control the coin, and through its agency works out his plans. Let none be so easily deceived as to place confidence in any such tests. Let none belittle their experience by resorting to cheap devices for direction in important matters connected with the work of God. . . .

"Will it furnish us with experiences that will

glorify God, for us to decide what is His will by the dropping of a card or a coin, and observing how it falls? No, no. Such tests as this will spoil the religious experience of the one who adopts them. Everyone who depends upon such things for guidance, needs to be reconverted."

God knows that for the growth of our own religious experience we must develop the power to think and decide. Therefore He has placed the responsibility upon us. Of course it always frustrates us to some extent. We find it much easier to simply follow instructions than to think.

When I give assignments to college students I find that the ones calling forth the loudest protests are not the long lists of facts to memorize or the numerous pages to read, but those that require thought and creativity. If I ask the class to memorize the chronology of Paul's letters I hear mild groans, but no major frustrations. But when I ask the same group to express the main point of a Pauline passage through some creative vehicle of their own, such as a story, essay, picture, or poem, their sense of frustration becomes immediately evident. You see, thinking is hard work, but that is what God requires of us.

But as we have said, the Lord does not leave us without guidance. Here we again see the importance of the Bible for Christian decision-making. Notice that in the quotation above,

Ellen White mentions the necessity to establish
our decisions on the sure foundation of the Word
of God. She also speaks of the sensible principles
that He has laid down for the guidance of His
people. The Lord has given us something far
more important than the right answers to our
every question—He has provided us with principles to guide us in our thinking.

There are two key words in the process of
Christian decision-making that we are advocat-
ing. The first is *response,* and the second is *reflection.* First, one sees all Christian action primarily
as a response to God.* Christian action is personal and relational. Our response to God includes our relationship to others as well, for each
person is one of God's children. As Jesus says,
" 'As you did it to one of the least of these my
brethren, you did it to me' " (Matthew 25:40).
The Christian attempts in all actions to respond
to God in a way suitable to His free gift of salvation.

But our response is not simply spontaneous.
Appreciating what God has done for us does not
necessarily mean we will automatically respond
appropriately. Even though God wants us to develop the power to think and to do and thus
refrains from providing us with prepackaged
right answers, He recognizes that we need guidance. Therefore He has revealed to us the princi-

ples that should govern our relationships with Him and others. Our decision-making reflects on those principles in the light of our particular time, place, and issue.

Thus Christian decision-making is a process of critical reflection that makes use of the guidance God has given in His Word. While our reason is not autonomous, neither is it idle. We attempt to see our situation in light of the principles of God's Word and after careful thought decide what course of action would be the most fitting response to God.

The next three chapters will explore the ways that Scripture gives guidance to us in the process of critical reflection and decision-making. Our reflection receives direction from the nature of the gospel as revealed in Scripture (Chapter 4), from the principles contained in the law (Chapter 5), and from the total Inspired Record of God's dealings with His people, a record reaching its climax in the story of God's supreme revelation in Christ (Chapter 6).

---

*Those acquainted with H. R. Niebuhr's typology of three ethical models presented in his *The Responsible Self: An Essay in Christian Moral Philosophy*, Intro. by James M. Gustafson (New York: Harper and Row, 1963), will notice our indebtedness to Niebuhr at this point. Niebuhr's three models are (1) Deontology, or an ethic of the right that asks,

"What is the law?" (2) Teleology, or an ethic of the good that asks, "What is the goal?" (3) An ethic that asks, "What is happening?" and, "What is the fitting response to what is happening?" Clearly the understanding of Christian decision-making presented here is closest to the third model, which Niebuhr advocates, but it is not identical with it. We understand the response in a much more specific way. It is not Niebuhr's more general response to all that is happening but a specific one of faith or trust in a personal God who has acted to save us freely in Jesus Christ.

Chapter 4

Walking Straight With the Gospel

When asked for a Biblical definition of sin, any self-respecting Seventh-day Adventist has the answer on the tip of his/her tongue: "Sin is the transgression of the law" (1 John 3:4, KJV). But Paul offers another statement about sin that we should not ignore, for it is both profound and provocative. In Romans 14:23 he says, "Whatever does not proceed from faith is sin."

Paul believes that if one grasps the Good News of salvation and responds by trusting God, it will make a difference in the life and actions. The Christian's actions will spring from trust or faith. Faith has implications for the life. That is why Paul can also say, "Lead a life worthy of the calling to which you have been called" (Ephesians 4:1), and "let your manner of life be worthy of the gospel of Christ" (Philippians 1:27).

Knowing the Good News of our calling has inevitable consequences in our everyday decisions. In fact, Paul often devotes the first part of his letters to a presentation of the Christian gospel and then moves to the ethical duties. He marks the transition from one section to the other with the word *therefore*. The second part is the consequence of the first. The equation thus becomes:

   a. the good news of salvation;

   b. therefore:

   c. these particular kinds of actions.

For examples of the "therefore" transition see Romans 12:1; Galatians 5:1; Ephesians 4:1.

Paul is saying that one's response to God has implications for the kind of life he/she lives. Faith becomes a spring from which actions flow, and whatever does not arise from that source is sin. Sin is not simply performing actions that are not "right" according to the law, but rather it's failing to live a life that emerges from faith and is consistent with the gospel. Thus the gospel provides not only the framework in which we stand as we make decisions (as we saw in Chapter 2) but it also has specific implications for the actual decisions we make. Therefore our process of critical reflection must begin with the gospel.

What we have said thus far may still seem rather abstract. Perhaps it would help to look at a concrete example from Paul's writings. In Galatians 2:11-14 he records an incident that had occured some years earlier in Antioch. In it and his subsequent comments on it we see how Paul considered certain actions to be inconsistent with the gospel.

Paul and Barnabas had been working in Antioch. There a type of Christianity first developed in which Jewish Christians and those converted from the pagan world actually joined together in one fellowship. Christians sat down at the same table and ate together, even though sharing a meal with non-Jews violated the tradition of many Jews. As Peter says in Acts 10:28, "You yourselves know how unlawful it is for a Jew to associate with or to visit anyone of another nation."

Other sources attest to the tradition as well. In a Jewish work called *Jubilees*, probably written in the second century BC, God instructs Jacob, "And do thou, my son Jacob, remember my words, And observe the commandments of Abraham, thy father: Separate thyself from the nations, And eat not with them." [1]

Mention of the refusal of Jews to eat with anyone of another nation also appears in non-Jewish sources, although it is difficult to know where truth stops and exaggeration begins. Diodorus, writing in the first century BC, says that the Jews "made their hatred of mankind into a tradition, and on this account had introduced utterly outlandish laws: not to break bread with any other race, nor to show them any good will at all." [2]

Thus the practice of the early Christians at Antioch went against some deep-seated traditions, and it was inevitable that it would cause controversy.

The apostle Peter came to Antioch, possibly to observe the new and revolutionary development in the church. We do not know whether he had any initial suspicions or not, but once he observed the situation he joined in eating with the Gentile believers, and as the tense of the Greek verb for "ate" in Galatians 2:12 shows, he did so not simply on one occasion but habitually.

But then a new group arrived in Antioch. Unfortunately, we do not know much about them. Paul simply calls them "certain men . . . from James." "James" was probably the Lord's brother and leader of the church at Jerusalem. Paul does not spell out their precise relationship to James. We do not know if they actually worked under his direction or had merely been associated with him. At any rate, they did not approve of the arrangement in Antioch.

No evidence indicated they demanded that the Gentile believers be circumcised and become Jews, but they obviously did not believe that Jews and Gentiles should eat together, even if they did share a common belief in Christ. They probably demanded a "separate but equal" policy in which both Jewish and Gentile believers would be accepted as Christians but would fellowship separately. In the wake of their criticism Peter withdrew and refused to continue taking meals with the Gentile believers. Even Barnabas, Paul's companion, went along and withdrew.

Paul says nothing of the reasoning that led Peter and Barnabas to their decision, but it is not hard to come up with some guesses. After all, wouldn't it be better not to offend those who simply could not accept such a radical departure from a revered tradition? And think of the difficulties that such fellowship would make for Jewish Christians who had non-Christian relatives. The non-Christian relatives would consider Jewish Christians who ate with Gentiles as unclean. Thus the practice would offend many people, both Christian and non-Christian. How much easier it would be to back off and remain separate from the Gentile believers in worship services and meals.

But Paul unrelentingly rejects the actions of Peter and Barnabas. He not only rebukes Peter publicly to his face but calls his action hypocritical and self-condemning. Notice what is especially important for our purposes in verse 14 (TEV*). Paul says that Peter and Barnabas "were not walking a straight path in line with the truth of the gospel."

At first his statement appears strange. We

would have no problem with the idea of believing, understanding, rejecting, or proclaiming the truth of the gospel, but what does it mean to walk straight with it?

For Paul the gospel is not simply an abstraction to believe. If the truth that God has freely saved him/her grasps one, it will make a difference in the way the individual walks through life. As we have said, the gospel has ethical implications. One rejects it not simply by refusing to believe its Good News but by failing to live in a way appropriate to it.

In this particular situation the gospel implied the necessity to recognize the unity of all believers in Christ and the obligation to express that unity by including all believers in the circle of church fellowship. To discriminate and refuse to accept another person contradicts the Good News that all people are saved solely on the basis of God's grace. To count the uncircumcised Gentile believers as second-class Christians, less than worthy of fellowship with their Jewish Christian counterparts, could not square with the truth that God's grace redeems all on an equal footing.

If God saves without making distinctions, for his followers to do so would not harmonize with His action. Thus Paul concluded that Peter and Barnabas were not walking in line with gospel truth. Consistency with the implications of the gospel demanded a certain course of action, and they failed to follow it because of their fear of other people.

Thus the truth of the gospel becomes a standard that guides the Christian as he/she reflects on his/her decisions. The Christian must ask, Is this course of action consistent with the gospel? If I truly believe that I have been redeemed by the God who makes no distinctions but saves all on the basis of faith, what differences will that make in my decision? When I am confronted with a situation in which I must choose between two possible actions, in what way would the truth of the gospel relate to each of the choices? Which alternative would best express my faith in a loving God?

The process is not as abstract as it may appear at first, for when a specific situation comes into view, such questions become instructive, as the incident recorded in Galatians 2 demonstrates. What a difference it would make if we examined all our decisions in the light of such questions. Consider what would happen, for instance, in our relationships with those of other races (even within the church).

The importance of Scripture's place in the process of studying the implications of the gospel for specific actions is obvious. First, Scripture explicates the Good News. For the Christian to receive the guidance that God offers, he/she must keep the Biblical presentation of the gospel continually in focus.

But Scripture not only unfolds the gospel, it also gives examples, both positive and negative, of the relationship between the Good News and the practical life. Through them we gain insights into the kinds of actions consistent with the gospel, as well as an understanding of their harmony. Finally, the Bible reveals specific principles implied by the gospel.

For instance, Paul states such a principle in Galatians 3:28 (a part of the same discussion that records the Antioch incident) when he concludes, "There is neither Jew nor Greek, there is neither slave nor free, there is neither male nor female; for you are all one in Christ Jesus." Thus we see an integral relationship between the gospel and particular decisions that we make, and a crucial role for the Bible in that relationship.

It would be a mistake, however, to limit the ethical implications of the gospel to its central truth, i.e., salvation by grace through faith in Jesus Christ. Although it is the great truth around which all others cluster, each of the doctrines of our faith has ethical implications. Paul makes use of many of them as he discusses practical questions of conduct for the believers in his churches.

For instance, in Romans 14:10-13 he can appeal to the doctrine of the judgment and show that one who truly believes that God will one day judge all men will hardly find it necessary to judge other people now. To believe in the judgment implies letting God be judge and not usurping His role. Thus the doctrine of the judgment has ethical implications. In Philippians 2 Paul appeals to the believers' understanding of Christology to show the humility that should govern the relationships between believers.

The relationship between what we believe and our daily decisions and actions is one of the most neglected aspects of Adventist theology. For example, we spend much more time arguing about the chronology of Creation or the question of the age of the earth than we do reflecting on the practical consequences of our belief that God is Creator.

What does the doctrine have to tell us about racial relations, the role of women in the church, or ecology? Certainly the Biblical account of Creation in Genesis 1-3 has important implications for such questions, implications that should help us make some important decisions on issues that confront us in both the church and society today.

To return for a moment to the introductory paragraph of the first chapter, our real need today is not to set aside the study of Bible doc-

trines or Christian beliefs in favor of concentrating on more relevant issues. Rather it is to focus
on Christian beliefs in such a way that we may
see their relevance for the crucial decisions that
confront us, for we need the guidance that God
offers us through such beliefs.

We should mention here one further aspect of
the relationship between belief and life-style.
When Paul begins to spell out for his congrega-
tions the kinds of actions inconsistent with the
gospel, it is clear that the Ten Commandments,
or the moral law, play an important part. For
instance, in the passage surveyed in the previous
chapter, 1 Corinthians 8:1-11:1, the act of eating
food offered to idols is completely neutral. But in
the course of his discussion Paul shows that the
matter is different with the worship of idols and
sexual immorality. He makes it clear that his
acceptance of food dedicated to idols and his
teaching that all things are lawful does not give
license for either idolatry or adultery.

While most Hellenistic authors could advise
against sexual relations outside of marriage, but
then be tolerant of such actions,[3] Paul takes a
much firmer stand. For him the law reveals certain kinds of actions that have negative effects on
one's relationships to God and to others. It points
to that which is inconsistent with faith. The
Christian does not set the law aside. It serves an

important function in Christian decision-making. And yet at the same time it is not the letter, but the spirit, that gives life.

Now we come to our next major question: What is the role of the law in Christian decision-making? Already we have said that it does not simply give right answers for every situation, but what is its function? Let us survey the second aspect of the role that the Bible plays in our process of decision-making as we turn to the part the Ten Commandments play.

---

[1] Jubilees 22:16, quoted in R. H. Charles, editor, *The Apocrypha and Pseudepigrapha of the Old Testament,* 2 vols. (Oxford: Clarendon Press, 1913), Vol. 2, p. 46.

[2] Menehem Stern, *Greek and Latin Authors on Jews and Judaism,* Vol. 1, *From Herodotus to Plutarch* (Jerusalem: The Israel Academy of Sciences and Humanities, 1976), p. 182, quoting from *Bibliotheca Historica* 34:1:1-5.

[3] For example, Epictetus says, "In your sex-life preserve purity, as far as you can, before marriage, and, if you indulge, take only those privileges which are lawful. [He refers to licensed prostitutes.]" Epictetus, *Encheiridion* 8, in *Epictetus,* trans. W. A. Oldfather, 2 vols. (New York: G. P. Putnam's Sons, 1926, 1928), vol. 2, p. 519.

[*] From The Bible in Today's English Version. Copyright, American Bible Society, 1976.

Chapter 5

"But I Say Unto You"

I had just begun my work as a student colporteur after my freshman year of college. It was a new experience in several ways. Never before had I been so far away from home, nor had I ever done that kind of work. I must admit the first few days were not too successful in terms of actually selling books. But then after a few days of finding out how much I needed to learn, an older, experienced colporteur came to help and teach me. The plan was that I would go with him, keep quiet, and watch to see how he did it. By now I was ready for his help.

At one of the first homes we met a woman who was greatly interested in the set of books we showed. It happened to be a five-volume set of Bible stories called *The Bible Pageant,* by Merlin Neff. She not only decided to buy but went and got the money to pay cash. But then as she started to hand it to us, she hesitated for a moment and said, "Before I get these books there is one thing I need to ask. About a year ago I almost bought another set of Bible stories I liked very much. There were ten of them, they were blue, and were written by a man named Maxwell. But I found out that they were put out by Seventh-day Adventists, and I wouldn't want anything in my house from them. Tell me, did Seventh-day Adventists publish these books?"

The colporteur opened one of the volumes to the title page, pointed to the bottom, and said, "Why, you can see right here that these books are put out by the Pacific Press Publishing Association." He then took the money, gave her the books, and we left.

At the time I remained silent as we had agreed (although I have since regretted that), but as soon as we left I began to question the colporteur. "What is she going to think when she finds out that Pacific Press is an Adventist publisher? Wasn't that lying to her?" The man replied that he had not lied. Everything that he told her was the truth. He had only said that Pacific Press published the books, which was true.

His statement presents a certain view of law. According to this approach (we will call it the literalistic view of law) one keeps the law by making sure that every action is in literal harmony with the law, and one breaks it by perform-

ing an act that the law forbids. As long as you are
in literal compliance, you are all right, but if you
are not, you are a lawbreaker.

But both the Old Testament presentation of
the Ten Commandments and the teachings of
Jesus demonstrate the inadequacy of the literalistic concept.

When we look at the Ten Commandments we
find that they do not concern themselves with
mere acts as acts, but with relationships. Sig-
nificantly the ninth commandment does not say,
"You shall not make any statement which does
not literally correspond with reality." Rather it
declares, "You shall not bear false witness *against
your neighbor*" (italics supplied). The commandment is concerned not with the act only but
with the relationship to the neighbor. The ninth
commandment is not ultimately about *statements*, but it is about *people* and the interactions
between them. Observing the commandment is
not just a matter of always making statements
that correspond with reality. One can do that and
still break the law.

Keeping the commandment means having
enough care and respect for another person to
honor his/her right to the truth. Obviously one
can deny truth to another without ever making a
false statement. The colporteur incident proves
that. One honors this commandment only by

being *for the neighbor* and respecting him/her enough to be genuinely truthful. Thus we see clues in the law itself that show us we should understand the law not in a literalistic but relational way.

Another clue comes at the beginning of the Ten Commandments—a vital part that we usually leave out when we have our children memorize them. God prefaces them with the words: "I am the Lord your God, who brought you out of the land of Egypt, out of the house of bondage" (Exodus 20:2). Deliverance from Egypt was *the* great sign of God's free gift of salvation in the Old Testament. Thus the Lord begins the commandments by reminding us that our obedience to the law is a *response* to God's free gift. Again it points up the relational nature of the law. The law is concerned with how we acknowledge God's saving love, not merely with the specific acts that we perform.

Jesus shows even more clearly the inadequacy of a literalistic view. In Matthew 5, where Jesus contrasts what the people have heard of old with His "I say unto you," He teaches that we do not break the law merely by acting out of harmony with its specific commands. To lust is to break the commandment that says, "You shall not commit adultery," and to hate is to break the command that says, "You shall not kill."

If we understand the law in a literalistic way, then refraining from the act of adultery or murder is keeping the law. But if the law is an explication of principles that will govern the relationships of one who has truly understood and accepted God's grace, any failure to be true to one of the most important commitments of life—the marriage vow—even if only in thought, and any failure to love are violations of the principle of the law.

Jesus' disputes with the Pharisees over the Sabbath point up the same truth. The Pharisees' literalistic view of law said, "The commandment says not to work, therefore if we make sure we refrain from any activity that might be considered work on the Sabbath, we will have kept the law." But Jesus saw true Sabbath observance as more than a matter of activity. He saw it in terms of relationships with God and others. For Him at certain times the basic principle of the law demanded that which they would have considered "work." It was not possible to love and at the same time let a person suffer rather than "work" on the Sabbath.

Jesus had no sympathy for a literalistic view of the Sabbath law. His Sabbathkeeping was not that of the ultraconservative Jews who had separated themselves from the rest of the people and gone out to the wilderness near the Dead Sea in search of purity. They would not lift an animal out of a pit or assist in the birth of an animal on Sabbath.[1] Nor was His Sabbath observance even like that of the more "liberal" Pharisees, who would lift an animal out of the pit but would not allow healing or the use of medications unless life was actually in danger.[2]

Jesus knew the truth of what Ellen White would later say in reflecting upon Jesus' actions: "God does not desire His creatures to suffer an hour's pain that may be relieved upon the Sabbath or any other day" (*The Desire of Ages,* p. 207).

We, of course, have recognized this in our own medical work. Once when I worked as a chaplain in an Adventist hospital I went to visit a non-Adventist who had just given birth to a new baby. Excited, she was eager to tell me all about her little girl. As she talked about how thankful she was that all had gone well, that the baby was healthy, and that it was a girl, she added, "and I'm so thankful that she came today. [It was Thursday.] She wasn't due for two more days, and I was worried sick. I wasn't sure what we were going to do if she was right on schedule. I heard that you don't deliver babies here on Saturdays."

Of course I assured her that we delivered babies whenever they decided to come. And we do so because we recognize that God never intended the law as a literalistic code but as the explication of principles which govern our relationship with Him and others.

Thus it is misleading to speak, as some do, of exceptions to the law, or of the necessity to "break" it in some situations. True, the obstetrician who delivers a baby on Sabbath is "working" in a sense, but that is breaking the Sabbath only if one interprets the words of the fourth commandment "In it you shall not do any work" in a literalistic sense. But according to Jesus we must look to the principle behind the command.

The obstetrician who must work by delivering a baby is actually observing the Sabbath by fulfilling his responsibility to God and others. For him to refuse his "work" would violate its principle. Thus the principle of the command to refrain from work on Sabbath might in some cases demand work, but that does not mean we are sometimes free to break the law. Rather, we *always* have the responsibility to be true to its basic principles. Only by fulfilling our responsibility do we truly observe the law.

Thus we see that we cannot regard the law as a literalistic code. If the law spoke only to the act itself in a literalistic way, the colporteur who deceived the woman by making a "true" statement would be a lawkeeper, while a husband who told his wife he was taking her to a business meeting when he was actually escorting her to a surprise party for her would be a lawbreaker. One cannot view any act apart from the network of relationships in which the one who acts stands, and it is those relationships, including one's relationship to God, to which the law speaks.

But once we have said all of this about the law, an objection will surely arise. Doesn't it open the floodgate to rationalization? How can a person be sure that he/she is not simply doing whatever he/she wants to do in the name of fulfilling the principles of the law? Can we really entrust humans with such responsibility and expect them to avoid rationalizing whatever they want to get away with?

First, people often overlook the fact that it is equally possible to rationalize with a literalistic view. Such an interpretation of law is vulnerable to the temptation to find loopholes in the law. A person can find many literalistic ways of getting around a law that he/she does not wish to obey. The Pharisees became experts at finding escape clauses that would enable them to retain their facade of carefully observing the law while at the same time doing as they pleased. They could play off one law against another, for example, by giving their belongings as a gift to God in order to

get around their responsibility to their parents
(see Mark 7 and Matthew 15). We fool ourselves if
we think that we can rationalize away our sins by
adhering to a literalistic observance of the law.

Second, understanding the law as principles
actually leads to greater responsibility and care
with regard to one's actions. No longer will mere
compliance with the letter of the law suffice. Nor
can one feel safe simply because "all these I have
observed from my youth." Now we must weigh
every action in the light of the law's principles. It
is not enough to just state technical truths, for we
must govern every relationship by principles of
honesty and a positive regard *for the neighbor*.

Instead of refraining from working on the
Sabbath, we let every act become the expression
of a positive response to the Creator, a desire to
fellowship with Him, a longing to love the other
children that He has created. It is the same with
each of the commandments. Instead of literalistic
rules to obey, we see them in *relational* terms.
They are windows into God's will that reveal the
principles governing our response to God and
the attitude to others appropriate in light of His
gift of grace to us.

How, then, do we make use of the law in our
actual decision-making? How is the process of
critical reflection about our action carried out in
relationship to the law?

Viewing the law as principles rather than literalistic rules means that the law is more like a book which grips us and helps to shape our values and our life than it is like a reference book we consult to find the answer to a specific question. (In fact, we could say the same of the Bible as a whole, as we will see in the following chapter.)

Every library has different kinds of books. In mine I have certain books that I would never think of reading through. They contain all sorts of facts that I would find difficult to carry around in my head all the time and most of which I probably don't care to know anyway. But some of the facts are useful on certain occasions, and thus I find the book itself of value. It sits on the shelf until needed, and then I consult it for the answer to a particular question.

Other books, however, have played a much different role in my life. Their contents have offered insights that have helped shape my understanding of myself and of the world around me. Some of them have had such a profound effect that I have returned to them again and again and have each time discovered new meaning. We often think of the law as a reference book that gives us the answer when we must decide what to do, but it is really much more like this other kind of work.

As we study and meditate on the law, its

principles mold the life. Our examination focuses not only on the Ten Commandments as such but on Jesus' teaching about the law and the way He lived in relationship to it. The law gives us insights into the nature of love for God and for others. Love for God becomes more than a nebulous feeling. We see that it includes recognizing that He alone is worthy of worship, respecting His name, and accepting the invitation to spend time with Him in the unique fellowship of the Sabbath.

Also we see that love for others is more than sentiment—it includes respect for life, property, truth, and the family relationship. And as the principles of love shape the life, we weigh individual decisions against them and search our motives in their light.

But even though the law gives specific character to love by revealing the principles that govern our relationships, it does not define the particular actions appropriate for every set of circumstances. God leaves that to us. Here again we see the necessity for reflection. For instance, while the law shows us that love demands honoring our parents, it does not stipulate which actions will honor them. That, of course, will differ from one occasion to another and from one culture to another. But from the law, I learn to ask of all my actions that relate to my parents, "Am I honoring them by a love consistent with God's love for me?"

Thus we cannot dispense with every difficult decision by simply consulting the law and "doing what it says." The law addresses us at a deeper level. It speaks to the motives that govern our relationships with God and others, and our critical reflection about individual decisions must begin with that. This is what the Bible means when it talks of the law's being written upon the heart. Through our meditation on the law and our contemplation of its significance we internalize the principles revealed in it so that they motivate our decisions and actions.

---

[1]The "Damascus Document" of the Dead Sea Scrolls instructs the Jewish sectarians, "No man shall assist a beast to give birth on the Sabbath day. And if it should fall into a cistern or pit, he shall not lift it out on the Sabbath" (G. Vermes, *The Dead Sea Scrolls in English,* second edition (Baltimore: Penguin Books, 1975), p. 113.

[2]The Mishnah, the codification of Jewish rabbinic teaching completed about the end of the second century AD, clearly forbids healing and the use of medicines on Sabbath. For example, Shabbath 14:4 holds that certain substances are not to be employed on Sabbath for medicinal purposes but may be employed in the customary nonmedical way so that the healing is not direct but is only a by-product. The passage reads:

"If his teeth pain him he may not suck vinegar through them but he may take vinegar after his usual fashion, and if he is healed he is healed. If his loins pain him he may not rub thereon wine or vinegar, yet he may anoint them with oil but not with rose-oil. King's children may anoint their wounds with rose-oil since it is their custom so to do on ordinary days" (Herbert Danby, trans., *The Mishnah* (Oxford: Clarendon Press, 1933), p. 113.

But the prohibition against Sabbath healing had an exception. If life was in danger before the Sabbath ended, healing was permitted. For instance, Yoma 8:6 says:

"If a man has a pain in his throat they may drop medicine into his mouth on the Sabbath, since there is doubt whether life is in danger, and whenever there is doubt whether life is in danger this overrides the Sabbath" (*ibid.*, p. 172).

Interestingly, Jesus chose to heal on Sabbath in cases where life was definitely not in danger. He healed a man who had been lame for thirty-eight years (John 5), a man born blind (John 9), a woman who had been ill for eighteen years (Luke 13: 11-17).

Chapter 6

Stories and Parables

For some time an often heated debate has taken place about the nature of God's revelation in Scripture. Over against those who see revelation only in experiential terms, conservative Christian theologians have emphasized the propositional nature of Scriptural revelation. Such emphasis is certainly both correct and needed. Scripture does reveal specific truths and commands.

Unfortunately, conservative Christians often fail to recognize or appreciate the fact that the Bible is by no means merely a collection of propositional statements. Sometimes we almost seem to wish that it were such a compilation. It would be so much more convenient if the Bible were more like *Bible Readings for the Home* with every doctrine laid out all ready for use in a Bible study. But God did not choose for His Word to come to us as a list of propositions and commands. Most

of the Bible is *stories,* and there is good reason for
that.

We live life as a story. Stories are the way we
experience reality. If asked to tell a new acquain-
tance a bit about who we are, we inevitably tell
accounts of our past experiences. Nothing
touches us where we actually live like a story.
Think of the last several sermons that you have
heard. What is it that you remember?

When I first began pastoring a church it used
to bother me that even the adults seemed to remember and pay closer attention to the children's story that I gave before the sermon than
they did to the sermon itself. I have since come to
recognize that fact as inevitable (and have thus
learned to include more stories in the sermon as
well). Jesus, of course, knew the value of a story.
That is one of the reasons he put much of his
teaching in parable.

Because we serve a personal God—a God who
is a person—the truth of who He is, what He has
done for us, and how we may appropriately respond to Him could not adequately be depicted
through a series of propositions and commands.
Only a personal revelation could reveal a personal God. Thus we see the supreme revelation
of God in Jesus.

And even the written revelation in Scripture
communicates the nature of God to us primarily

as a story of His actions for man and of man's response. Obviously if we limit Scripture's relevance for decision-making to specific commands, we rule out most of the Bible. But the process of critical reflection concerning our decisions can make use of the entire Bible.

Here again the role that Scripture plays in shaping the whole life and its values is even more significant than its part in providing right answers to specific dilemmas. Let's see how this is true by using the stories of Jesus' life as an example.

We can hardly concentrate on the stories of Jesus recorded in the Gospels without having our values challenged. Something happens to our way of thinking when we see His way of looking at people. We begin to ask ourselves certain questions. What kind of people did Jesus come in contact with? How did He treat them? How did they respond to Him? What does it all mean for the way I view people around me? Of what significance is it for me that He seemed to have much more patience with open sinners than with the pious saints who were always pointing the finger at them?

One can hardly contemplate the Biblical stories in a sympathetic way without developing a sensitivity for the oppressed and the open sinner. When we read the narratives with an awareness of who Jesus is and what God was doing for us in Him, they have the power to mold our values and patterns of thinking about other people.

Or think of the matter of one's attitude to money. We can hardly contemplate stories like the rich young ruler (Mark 10:17-22 and parallels), the widow's mite (Mark 12:41-44 and parallels), the foolish rich man (Luke 12:16-21), the rich man and Lazarus (Luke 16:19-31), or Zacchaeus (Luke 19:1-10) without having our values affected. And of course our values then affect the specific decisions that we make.

Every day we make choices about money. Probably few of them loom up before us as great ethical dilemmas, although at times we find ourselves forced to seriously contemplate specific ones in the light of the Biblical principles and stories that relate to the topic. But it is at least as important, if not more so, that the values inherent in the gospel story guide our everyday decisions about money.

Thus the Bible is relevant for our decision-making not only as it helps us make particular choices but also as it transforms the character or the kind of person we are, for that, in turn, conditions all of the future decisions that we make.

But the specific stories and incidents recorded in the Bible may also speak in a more direct way to the dilemmas that we face. We can look to them for guidance when we have a particular consideration or issue confronting us, but we cannot expect an instant relevance to free us from effort. In fact, danger exists that we may use stories and incidents in Scripture to justify almost any action. We have all seen cases in which two people have used the same Scriptural passages to advocate opposite courses of action. Consequently we need some kind of restraint lest we use Biblical stories to say almost anything.

Of course we can never have an absolute control guaranteeing that every person will agree on the relevance of a particular passage for a specific situation. We are not dealing with test tubes and computers here. But certain methods of Scriptural interpretation can help us avoid the temptation to read our own desires into the passage or to try and receive guidance from a passage that is not really relevant to the issue we face. This control comes as we study Scripture within its historical and literary context. It means that before we ask, "What is the relevance of the passage for my problem?" we must first ask, "What was the Biblical writer trying to say in *his* circumstance?" Before we inquire what a passage of Scripture *means* for us we must ask what it originally *meant* for the author and those to whom he wrote.

Consequently we need to know as much as

possible about the historical situation that stands behind the text. We also must carefully study the passage within its literary framework to try and discover the structure of the author's thought so that we can understand the actual point being made, as well as why he made it. Thus the historical and interpretive task serves as a necessary control when we use Scripture in our process of critical reflection about decisions.

We do not mean to say, of course, that only professional historians or Biblical scholars can benefit from Scripture. Common sense and careful observation will enable us to interpret Scripture most of the time, and where we especially need specific historical information, numerous sources commonly available today will provide it. On the other hand we must not reduce Bible study to a historical exercise that has as its goal merely to show what the author intended to say. If Bible study stops here, it may or may not be interesting, but it will certainly not be relevant. Rather the interpretative task opens the way for Scripture to speak to us in our modern circumstances.

Only when we have interpreted a text within its original historical and literary context can our reflection about what it means for us grow out of and be consistent with its actual intent. We are then free to begin comparing our situation with that addressed in the passage.

We can ask: To what extent is the issue confronting me similar to and/or different from that addressed in the text? To what extent can we generalize the story? Are there inherent principles that I should consider in my case? What was it about the decision the person in this story made that renders it an appropriate (or inappropriate) way of responding to God? Would a similar action on my part express the same motives? Would it have the some consequences?

What principles and values are at stake in the passage? Are they involved in the decision I must make, and if so, in what ways? What does the story reveal about God, and how would it be fitting to respond to such a God if I really put my trust in Him?

Admittedly such a process of interpretation and reflection takes effort. But it is only through such struggle and toil that we can (1) come to truly understand what Scripture is saying and (2) see its relevance for our own time. Ellen White wrote of Scripture study: "To skim over the surface will do little good. Thoughtful investigation and earnest, taxing study are required to comprehend it" (*Fundamentals of Christian Education*, p. 390).

In another passage she declared: "By Bible study and daily communion with Jesus we shall gain clear, well-defined views of individual responsibility and strength to stand in the day of trial and temptation. . . .

"The Christian is required to be diligent in searching the Scriptures, to read over and over again the truths of God's word. Willful ignorance on this subject endangers the Christian life and character" (*Testimonies*, Vol. 5, p. 273).

When we conduct this kind of diligent study we will see in a new perspective many passages of Scripture that might at first sight appear to have little relevance for our decision-making. For instance, in Chapter 3 we surveyed Paul's advice to the Corinthians concerning food offered to idols. A discussion of that topic could hardly seem to have any bearing on us. Not one of us has ever had to face the dilemma in the supermarket of whether we would purchase food that we knew to have been consecrated in a pagan temple.

But when we take time to understand the significance of the issue the Corinthians struggled with, to carefully observe *what* it is that Paul says and *why*, we find that much more is as stake than food offered to idols. We see that what is really involved is how Christians should relate to those whose backgrounds give them a different perspective on what is right and wrong, how one must respond when an action threatens to injure a weaker Christian, and how Christian freedom and responsibility must come together. Once we realize this, an irrelevant passage suddenly becomes important as we consider many decisions about how we will relate to other members of the church, for even though the problem of food offered to idols no longer troubles us, plenty of other problems between church members involve the same principles and values.

That which may seem to have no immediate relevance appears in a new light through diligent study and critical reflection. Thus the whole Bible, not just the specific commands and sections of moral instruction, guides the Christian in the decision-making process.

We should give one word of caution, however. One can use Scriptural stories for moral instruction in a way that circumvents the above process and robs them of their full power to speak to our lives. I am referring to our penchant for moralization. In moralization we take a story and draw a specific moral lesson from it. The problem is that usually the moral lesson is not what the author originally intended. Often we could obtain the moral lesson from any number of sources. Although we ignore the actual intent of Scripture, we think that we are being "Biblical" because it is something in the Bible that has suggested the point to us. But when we replace the author's point with our moralization, we are merely using Scripture as a springboard.

One of the particularly unfortunate things about moralization is it tends to keep us from getting all that the Biblical passage might have to say to us. Our examination of the passage ends with the general moral lesson, and we have no incentive to delve deeper, never seeing the actual principles and values at issue.

Unfortunately the tendency to moralize is still alive and well. It particularly appears when we employ the Bible in religious instruction for children. Such teaching often consists of telling the Biblical story and tacking on a moralization at the end. In fact, such morals often sound strangely alike. They all show what good girls and boys the children should be, But we seldom hear the real message of Scripture, for moral admonitions are not the gospel.

Let me give an example of what I mean. I recently saw a presentation of Jesus' cleansing the temple which ended with the warning that children should not whisper in church. What a sad fate for a story so rich with meaning to suffer. Much had been lost. And what very different issues were actually involved in the story.* But we rob our children of all that when we reduce the story to an admonition to be quiet in church. Such moralization degrades Scripture to an instrument of social control.

It is not by drawing easy moral lessons from Biblical stories that we will find their relevance for us but by carefully listening to them within their own literary and historical context to see what the author meant and then moving on to reflect on the significance of the issues and principles inherent within the story for our own circumstances. When we do so, our efforts will not go unrewarded. What we contemplate in Scripture will continually shape our characters, even our very lives, and in addition we will receive specific guidance for the decisions that confront us as we reflect on what we find in the Bible.

---

*It is not within the scope of our present discussion to explore the significance of the cleansing of the temple, but read chapter 16 of *The Desire of Ages* and notice some of the important issues at stake in this story, such as the person, role, and authority of Jesus, the oppression of the poor, the true nature of worship.

Chapter 7

Summary

At this point I am sure some readers feel dis-appointed that this has not been more of a "how-to-do-it" book on making decisions, that we have not given more assurance of the Bible's having a specific answer for every dilemma, or even that we have not stated that one can always be certain after going to the Bible that he/she has made the "right" decision. Rather we have found that Scripture is not a reference book to keep on the shelf until, confronted with a dilemma, we take it down, open it to the appropriate page, and presto—the right answer. But it does not mean that Scripture is not relevant for our decison-making. It is pertinent in a much more important way.

We must never forget that its most important function is revealing the gospel to us, for it is in the gospel that we find our salvation. Scripture does much more than tell us what to do. It liberates us from the illusion that our doing can save, from the tyranny of depending upon *our* activity. The Bible delivers us from the guilt of our past doing by freely offering us forgiveness. It rescues us from the plight of not doing even that which we know we should by offering us God's transforming love. And it frees us *for* a new life lived in response to God's gracious gift. What a tragedy it would be if we missed all of this and simply looked to the Bible for instruction about what to do! The significance of our doing becomes visible only in the light of what God has done.

But Scripture also gives guidance as we respond to God and attempt to live a life appropriate to His gift. It shows us that a loving relationship with God and others is the only appropriate response. In addition it gives specific character to this love by revealing a whole history of God's loving actions on behalf of man, and of man's response to them. The Bible demonstrates what love has meant in many specific instances, as well as the principles that will govern relationships truly based on love. Scriptural guidance is much more than a listing of the right answers to particular dilemmas—it speaks rather to the bases on which we make our decisions.

We have noted two ways that we appropriate the Bible's guidance in our lives. First, we as-

similate it through continual contemplation.
When we study Scripture as a response to a personal God, it shapes the values and principles by
which we live. As our character forms, our new
Bible-based values condition all of life's decisions. Thus the Bible plays a role in decision-
making that more resembles the process of re-
ceiving an education than of finding the answer
to a question in a reference book.

Second, we internalize the guidance Scripture offers through a process of critical reflection
that makes use of Scripture when confronting
specific decisions. This process first attempts to
understand those passages that appear to be
relevant within their historical and literary context so as to discover their original intent. It then
views the present in light of this intent, paying
particular attention to the kinds of values and
principles at stake in the Biblical account.

The truths of the gospel, the principles of love
revealed in the law, and the entire inspired story
of God's interaction with man—all provide help
and insight. And throughout, the one who reflects on his/her action in the light of Scripture
recognizes that salvation does not come from
making the correct decisions. Rather he/she
wants to do each time that which is most in
keeping with God's free gift of salvation, which
He has already given. Thus it is a process of

response and reflection,* and perhaps that would be the most appropriate label (if we need one) for the model of Christian decision-making presented here.

Such critical reflection is not necessarily easy. It in no way frees us from the effort of thinking and deciding, nor does it guarantee that all our decisions will be perfect. But as we reflect, decide, and act, we do have the assurance *that God is with us*. He does not make our decisions for us, but He does have the power to turn even our mistakes to good through His providence.

A parent might accompany a child who is learning to cross the street and refuse to tell him/her when to cross, but at the same time keep a careful eye lest a mistake spell disaster. Sometimes even after our best efforts at reflection, we still make the wrong choice, for human weakness keeps us from ever seeing all things perfectly. But God realizes that. He looks not only at our deeds but at the motives prompting them.

The Lord knows when we are acting out of genuine appreciation for what He has done. God understands when we attempt something out of love but end up bringing hurt because of our failure to read the situation properly. And He is even willing to forgive when selfishness mixes with our most loving deeds. When we realize all of this about God, we discover an assurance far greater than the promise of guaranteed right answers could ever provide.

Perhaps we can further summarize our model of response and reflection by briefly contrasting it with some of the other common approaches to Christian decison-making.

We have already discussed one popular concept detail in chapters 3 and 5. The "Just obey" model stresses that literalistic obedience to specific commands is the necessity of Christian duty. The Christian must not think or reason but only obey. However, the model has a number of problems. It fails to recognize that relationships are more important than acts in and of themselves, that the significance of acts may differ, depending on the circumstances, and that neither Scripture nor Ellen White speaks on many important moral problems. It also has a tendency to rationalize by finding loopholes in the specific commands. While it takes the guidance given in Scripture seriously, it spurns responsibility and oversimplifies Christian duty.

A second model is the "Just love" approach. It stresses that love is to motivate all Christian actions. Thus if the Christian will only love, one may do as he/she pleases. One need not worry about rules or laws. The only law is love. The problem that arises is that one can forget the true character of Christian love and reduce it to just a nebulous feeling unless he/she has sufficient input from Scripture. Love can all too easily come to mean nothing more than that which we feel like doing.

Here again rationalization becomes a dominant temptation, although its nature is different from that of the "Just obey" model. Here rationalization comes through excusing actions on the basis of loving motives. Often one gives insufficient attention to the consequences of actions. One tends to forget that justice is a part of love. And while the model gives a serious place to responsibility, it downgrades the guidance that God has provided in Scripture.

A third model is the "What would Jesus do?" concept. In each situation the Christian asks what Jesus would do in his/her circumstances and acts accordingly. But it has many of the same problems as the "Just love" model. It becomes easy to read our own desires into our assessment of what Jesus would do. The temptation to make Jesus according to our own image is almost unavoidable. That is why often no two opinions about what Jesus would do in a given incident are the same. Rather than trying to guess what Jesus would do, it is far more important that we become sensitive to the values and principles inherent in what Jesus actually did as we focus on Scripture.

The fourth and final model that we will mention is the "Let the Spirit lead" viewpoint. Here the Christian simply follows the promptings of the Spirit, depending upon Him for daily guidance. Its problem is one of criteria. How does one distinguish the urging of the Spirit from his/her own desires? Is that dream, which seemed to indicate the answer to some problems, the Spirit speaking or the result of last night's big dinner? How does one differentiate the Spirit's from other voices?

I will never forget talking with someone who told me that the Spirit had told him to kill someone! How do we know which spirit is working? Letting the Spirit lead might be nothing more than being controlled by circumstances.

We do not minimize the work of the Spirit. Through Him God is present with us. The Spirit works in our lives to transform our thinking and bring it into harmony with God, and through Him we receive His power in our lives. But the Spirit uses *Scripture* to accomplish His task.

While we can never expect to understand Scripture without the aid of the Spirit and should never open the Bible without asking for His guidance, we can also never expect to sit back and have the Spirit make our decisions for us or have Him drop from the sky the right answer to every decision that confronts us. To the extent that we ignore and neglect God's revelation in Scripture we deny ourselves of the criteria for recognizing the Spirit's voice as well as of the means by which He addresses us.

The model we have suggested, that of response to God's grace and of reflection on our decisions, attempts to avoid many of the pitfalls of the four above. It accepts responsibility but at the same time takes seriously the specific guidance God has given in Scripture. Recognizing that actions receive significance only as they affect relationships with God and others, it also realizes that the specific principles revealed in the law are necessary for maintaining the proper relationships.

The model knows that the act is not as important as the love that motivates it, but it looks to Scripture to see the specific character of that love. Finally it sees faith as the spring from which Christian action flows while remembering that faith must seek guidance by reflecting on the principles contained in God's Word.

We will conclude this chapter by returning once more to the incident reported at the beginning of the book. Now that we have explored the role of the Bible in Christian decision-making, what would I say to my fellow educator who asked the question about "Biblical" and "relevant" courses? Actually I can sympathize with his question, for I share with him the concern for relevance.

If we present the Bible as a mere history book and the goal of its study is only to find out what the author intended to say or to develop neat lists of proof texts to support doctrines, we might well question its value for us today.

At the same time, if we simply put the Bible aside in favor of "relevant" issues, we are the losers, even if we come to the Bible for help with them. Unless we let Bible principles *continually* shape our lives, we will lack the experience of faith that lies at the foundation of Christian decision-making, and unless we study Scripture systematically and diligently, we will overlook much in it that is vital for our decisions.

We conclude that we can be both Biblical and relevant. In fact, we cannot really be relevant in a Christian way without being Biblical, for only in the light of Scripture do we find the basic framework of and the specific principles for Christian decision-making.

We now turn to some examples of the process of reflecting on specific situations in the light of the Scripture.

---

*The purpose of this book has been to explore the place of the Bible in this process of reflection, but it does not suggest that the Bible is the only source for Christian reflection.

Because the Christian reflects on the principles of the Scriptures *as they relate to his/her case*, anything that enlightens the problem must also come into view. Psychological, sociological, historical, or anthropological information might help, for example. In addition, if we take our doctrine of Creation seriously, the same God who reveals Himself in the Scriptures also created the world. Thus we should be able to learn from the world around us, both natural and human, as well. But His Word is always the norm by which we evaluate all the other sources.

Chapter 8

Some Examples

The previous chapter brought an end to the actual argument of this book. This chapter provides some specific examples for your reflection. They are not hypothetical but actual ones faced by Christians. The goal of the chapter is to involve you in reflection, not to solve the problems. In fact, we have tried to avoid the temptation of giving our own views lest you see the goal of the chapter in terms of the result rather than process. (Human beings have a tendency to stop thinking once they have received an answer.) Perhaps you will find this chapter profitable not only for personal reflection but for group discussion as well.

The procedure is as follows: First we will present a problem that demands some kind of decision. Then we will give several passages of Scripture (and in one case a quotation from the writings of Ellen White) that might be relevant to the decision. For the sake of convenience we have printed them out in their entirety. Your task is to reflect on the passages and see how they might give guidance in the specific situation. We will only ask a few questions for each of the passages to help get the process of reflection started. From there on you are on your own.

It is our hope that this will aid in suggesting the shape that the process of your thinking might take as it makes use of specific scriptures. At the same time the reader must remember that we cannot limit the relevance of Scripture for these decisions to the two or three specific passages presented here.

Example One
The circumstance:

On an Adventist college campus, students largely depend on the college cafeteria for their meals. It serves three meals each day except Sabbath, when in an attempt to save work, it omits breakfast. In lieu of Sabbath breakfast the cafeteria provides various breakfast foods, including cereal, to the students as they go through line for the evening meal on Friday.

Milk is also available, but many students do not have any way of keeping milk cold overnight in their rooms, so they prefer to get it on Sabbath morning from the milk machines in the dormitories. However, not comfortable with the idea of purchasing milk on Sabbath, the deans in one of the dorms decide that they should close the vending-machine room during the Sabbath hours. The deans in the other dorm see no problem with the students' buying milk from vending machines on Sabbath and leave their rooms open.

The difference in practice between the two dorms brings the issue to the forefront, and it becomes a major item of debate all over the campus. Battle lines form, and everywhere one hears arguments why it is right or wrong to buy and sell milk in vending machines on Sabbath. Obviously no vending machines existed when the Bible was written. Thus no text of Scripture gives a simple answer to the question. Should the milk machines be opened or closed on Sabbath? Passages for reflection:

1. Exodus 20:8-11: "Remember the sabbath day, to keep it holy. Six days you shall labor, and do all your work; but the seventh day is a sabbath to the Lord your God; in it you shall not do any work, you, or your son, or your daughter, your manservant, or your maidservant, or your cattle, or the sojourner who is within your gates; for in six days the Lord made heaven and earth, the sea, and all that is in them, and rested the seventh day; therefore the Lord blessed the Sabbath day and hallowed it."

Does the fourth commandment give any help on the question? The commandment explicitly forbids "work" on the Sabbath. What constitutes work? Is the matter of work involved in any way in the question about milk machines? In what way would the opening or closing of the machines add or detract from the principles of Sabbathkeeping presented in the commandment?

2. Mark 2:23-28: "One sabbath he was going through the grainfields; and as they made their way his disciples began to pluck heads of grain. And the Pharisees said to him, 'Look, why are they doing what is not lawful on the sabbath?' And he said to them, 'Have you never read what David did, when he was in need and was hungry, and he and those who were with him: how he entered the house of God, when Abiathar was high priest, and ate the bread of the Presence, which it is not lawful for any but the priests to eat, and also gave it to those who were with him?' And he said to them, 'The sabbath was made for man, not man for the sabbath; so the Son of man is lord even of the sabbath.'

Are there any similarities between the episode of the disciples in the grainfields and that of the students in the dormitories? Are the reasons for the disciples' eating the same as those of the students for buying milk? Are there any differences between the two incidents? Is the fact significant that one case involves money and the other does not? Since God made the Sabbath for man, does it leave each one free to decide such questions for himself/herself, or are there limits to the freedom that this text seems to imply? What are the basic principles at stake in the Biblical story? How do they relate to the problem of the milk machine?

3. Romans 14:1–15:7: "As for the man who is weak in faith, welcome him, but not for disputes over opinions. One believes he may eat anything, while the weak man eats only vegetables. Let not him who eats despise him who abstains, and let not him who abstains pass judgment on him who eats; for God has welcomed him. Who are you to pass judgment on the servant of another? It is before his own master that he stands or falls. And he will be upheld, for the Master is able to make him stand.

"One man esteems one day as better than another, while another man esteems all days alike. Let every one be fully convinced in his own mind. He who observes the day, observes it in honor of the Lord. He also who eats, eats in honor of the Lord, since he gives thanks to God. None of us lives to himself, and none of us dies to himself. If we live, we live to the Lord, and if we die, we die to the Lord; so then, whether we live or whether we die, we are the Lord's. For to this end Christ died and lived again, that he might be Lord both of the dead and of the living.

"Why do you pass judgment on your brother? Or you, why do you despise your brother? For we shall all stand before the judgment seat of God; for it is written, 'As I live, says the Lord, every knee shall bow to me; and every tongue shall give praise to God.' So each of us shall give account of himself to God.

"Then let us no more pass judgment on one another, but rather decide never to put a stumbling block or hindrance in the way of a brother. I know and am persuaded in the Lord Jesus that nothing is unclean in itself; but it is unclean for any one who thinks it unclean. If your brother is being injured by what you eat, you are no longer walking in love. Do not let what you eat cause the ruin of one for whom Christ died. So do not let your good be spoken of as evil. For the kingdom of God is not food and drink but righteousness and peace and joy in the Holy Spirit; he who thus serves Christ is acceptable to God and approved by men.

"Let us then pursue what makes for peace and for mutual upbuilding. Do not, for the sake of food, destroy the work of God. Everything is indeed clean, but it is wrong for any one to make others fall by what he eats; it is right not to eat meat or drink wine or do anything that makes your brother stumble. The faith that you have, keep between yourself and God; happy is he who has no reason to judge himself for what he approves. But he who has doubts is condemned, if he eats, because he does not act from faith; for whatever does not proceed from faith is sin.

"We who are strong ought to bear with the failings of the weak, and not to please ourselves; let each of us please his neighbor for his good, to edify him. For Christ did not please himself; but, as it is written, 'The reproaches of those who reproached thee fell on me.' For whatever was written in former days was written for our instruction, that by steadfastness and by the encouragement of the scriptures we might have hope. May the God of steadfastness and encouragement grant you to live in such harmony with one another, in accord with Christ Jesus, that together you may with one voice glorify the God and Father of our Lord Jesus Christ.

"Welcome one another, therefore, as Christ has welcomed you, for the glory of God."

At first sight the inclusion of this passage may appear strange, for it has nothing to do with the Sabbath. Thus a word of explanation is in order. Here Paul addresses a church in which the "weak" and "strong" Christians had divided over a question of food and days, probably vegetarianism (which in this context has nothing to do with health) and the observance of fast days.

As Paul speaks to the situation, he never gives a "right answer" to the question with which all members must comply (although he does identify with the strong). Rather, he concentrates on the way those who differ on the specifics should relate to each other. The "strong" should not scorn the weak and look down their noses at them for being so particular. The "weak" should not judge the strong because their standards are more "liberal" and permit that which the weak consider wrong. Both should accept each other as Christ has accepted them. Thus the possible relevance of the passage comes not because it speaks to the question of the Sabbath but because it addresses a case in which Christians had split over specific decisions.

Is the question of the milk machines like that of days and foods at Rome, one in which the way those who differ over the issue relate to each other is more important than the issue itself? Or is the situation here one calling for a specific right answer with which everyone complies? What specific factors make the two incidents similar and/or different? Would Paul's advice that each should be fully convinced in his own mind apply here? Are there principles implicit in his advice that might be important for any question dividing Christians over an issue of specific practice? Finally, can you think of other Scriptures that might be relevant for reflection?

Example Two
The circumstances:

During World War II some Adventist Christians learned what was happening to Jews in Germany. Living on the German border, they became aware of underground groups who were assisting Jews to escape from Germany, men, women, and children almost certainly earmarked for death. The underground groups sought the aid of these Christians. In order to facilitate the escape of Jews they would help prepare false identification records and participate in other actions intended to deceive the border guards. The difficulty of the decision was that if they did not assist they would be failing to act to save lives, but if they did, they would be involved in deception. Should they have participated?
Passages for reflection:

1. Exodus 20:16: "You shall not bear false witness against your neighbor."

Would the deception of the border guards be bearing false witness against the neighbor? Who is the neighbor in this incident? Does the commandment forbid all deception, or would circumstances make a difference? To what extent should they respect the guards' right to truth? Is the use that the guards would make of the truth a factor in the Christian decision?

2. Exodus 20:13: "You shall not kill."

Does the command against killing include a positive command to preserve life? If those who might have escaped were subsequently executed because the Christian refused to participate, would he/she share in the responsibility for the killing? To what extent should one leave such results with God and avoid deception at all costs? Does Christian responsibility demand active participation for the sake of preserving life?

3. Exodus 1:15-21: "Then the king of Egypt said to the Hebrew midwives, one of whom was named Shiprah and the other Puah, 'When you serve as midwife to the Hebrew women, and see them upon the birthstool, if it is a son, you shall kill him; but if it is a daughter, she shall live.' But the midwives feared God, and did not do as the king of Egypt commanded them, but let the male children live. So the king of Egypt called the midwives and said to them, 'Why have you done this, and let the male children live?' The midwives said to Pharoah, 'Because the Hebrew women are not like the Egyptian women; for they are vigorous and are delivered before the midwife comes to them.' So God dealt well with the midwives; and the people multiplied and grew

very strong. And because the midwives feared God he gave them families."

4. Joshua 2:1-14: "And Joshua the son of Nun sent two men secretly from Shittim as spies, saying, 'Go, view the land, especially Jericho.' And they went, and came into the house of a harlot whose name was Rahab, and lodged there. And it was told the king of Jericho, 'Behold, certain men of Israel have come here tonight to search out the land.' Then the king of Jericho sent to Rahab, saying, 'Bring forth the men that have come to you, who entered your house; for they have come to search out all the land.' But the woman had taken the two men and hidden them; and she said, 'True, men came to me, but I did not know where they came from; and when the gate was to be closed, at dark, the men went out; where the men went I do not know; pursue them quickly, for you will overtake them.' But she had brought them up to the roof, and hid them with the stalks of flax which she had laid in order on the roof. So the men pursued after them on the way to the Jordan as far as the fords; and as soon as the pursuers had gone out, the gate was shut.

"Before they lay down, she came up to them on the roof, and said to the men, 'I know that the Lord has given you the land, and that the fear of you has fallen upon us, and that all the inhabitants of the land melt away before you. For we have heard how the Lord dried up the water of the Red Sea before you when you came out of Egypt, and what you did to the two kings of the Amorites that were beyond the Jordan, to Sihon and Og, whom you utterly destroyed. And as soon as we heard it, our hearts melted, and there was no courage left in any man, because of you; for the Lord your God is he who is God in heaven above and on earth beneath.

" 'Now then, swear to me by the Lord that as I have dealt kindly with you, you also will deal kindly with my father's house, and give me a sure sign, and save alive my father and mother, my brothers and sisters, and all who belong to them, and deliver our lives from death.' And the men said to her, 'Our life for yours! If you do not tell this business of ours, then we will deal kindly and faithfully with you when the Lord gives us this land.' "

Do the Hebrew midwives and Rahab provide a positive example of deception in order to save a life? Does it make any difference that Rahab was a non-Israelite? Would God have expected His people to act differently, or would He have wanted them to do as Rahab did? What do you see as the main point of the stories? Is that message relevant for the problem under consideration? In what ways?

5. *Testimonies*, Vol. 4, p. 336: "Even life

itself should not be purchased with the price of falsehood.''

Does Mrs. White's statement settle the issue? Would it seem to condemn the actions of Rahab and the midwives, praised in the Bible? Would the fact that it is someone else's life rather than one's own make a difference? Does Ellen White intend to speak to the kind of incident presented here? Does the context of the statement (a discussion of martyrs who could have gotten themselves freed by a word or nod) affect the relevance of the statement for this issue? Again, can you think of any other passages that might bear on the question?